A Childhood in the Woods

By Mary Bratman

Illustrated and Edited by Roger Neumaier

Introduction

Mary Bratman was my grandmother. Born in 1901 and raised on her parent's farm which was carved out of forest near Rib Lake in Northern Wisconsin, she saw a side of life that few who are now living have experienced.

In 1961, when my sixth-grade class was studying the settlers of Minnesota, our teacher, Mrs. DuCharme, gave me and my classmates a list of questions to ask of parents and grandparents. Those questions are included as an appendix in the back of this book. My grandmother responded by writing a wonderful recollection of her childhood. Few edits have been made to her response and, while I do not claim to be an artist, I added illustrations to her words to help younger readers visualize her story.

A Childhood in the Woods shares Mary Bratman's vibrant childhood memories not only with her descendants but also with other young people who are curious about life in this country at a simpler time.

This book is dedicated to my grandmother, Mary Bratman. I hope you will enjoy her delightful description of a childhood in the woods.

Roger Neumaier, February, 2025

Great grandfather and great grandmother lived in Passaic New Jersey. In the year of 1899, they moved to Wisconsin. Great grandfather wanted to be a lumberman. When they left New Jersey, they had two sons. Uncle Henry was three years and Uncle Ed was one year old.

It was a long train ride as trains then were very slow.

The boys got the measles on the trip. Great grandmother was still in her teens and also contracted measles. When they came to their destination to live with a relative, you can imagine the welcome they received.

All that was there was wilderness.

Great grandfather cut down trees and used the logs to build a one room cabin. Between the logs he put mud and marsh hay. That was the home's plaster. The cabin was heated with a wood stove. But it was not warm and the family had to watch the fire to keep the cabin from burning or becoming too hot. Even at night, they had to take turns keeping the fire going.

Great grandfather went to work in the woods as a lumberman. He did not know the trade. So, the first thing he did was chop his leg. Things ended up with four sick people and very little money.

There were no doctors nearby and no highways — only a trail through the woods. To get food they had to walk five miles.

Great grandfather was a good hunter. When he hunted, he always brought home some type of game like rabbits, partridge and deer. All he would have to do was open the log cabin door and shoot. Game was plentiful.

In the summer we would pick blueberries, raspberries and cherries. In the fall we would find a lot of cranberries.

We also would pick ground pine, little greens that grew like a Christmas tree. These were tied in bundles like a bouquet and put in big sacks to be sold.

With the money, great grandfather and great grandmother would buy food and clothing.

That same year, great grandfather bought some land and began farming.

He still worked in the woods most of the time. Logs were hauled to the mill for lumber. In the middle of summer, he made money peeling bark. When big trees were cut down, the bark was also sent to the mills.

After they had farmed a while, great grandpa and great grandma had potatoes and vegetables to eat.

They needed a cellar or root house to store their harvest. Great grandpa dug a deep hole in the ground. In the bottom of the hole, he laid marsh hay. Then he put small logs across the pit. On top of the logs, he put more marsh hay and then earth on top of the hay so it looked like a hill. He made a door of smaller logs.

An opening was left on the side of the hill for this door. After he put the door on the root house, he covered it with hay and earth.

The cellar was big enough for us to walk around in.

When we needed vegetables all we had to do was start digging. With the cabbage, they made a lot of sauerkraut. Great grandmother always had sauerkraut cooking on the stove. When we got tired of plain sauerkraut, we made sauerkraut sandwiches.

When we butchered wild game or a pig, we would share some of the meat with neighbors. The neighbors would also share with us when they had meat. Deer were always divided with others. Meats could be canned and we also made sausage. We would smoke bacon and hams. With a large family, the meat was used up faster.

When milk spoiled, we would make cottage cheese.

If we wanted a small amount of butter, we would take a two-quart jar, fill it half full of cream and just shake it. In a short time, it would turn into butter.

We also had a barrel type butter churn. It had a wooden cover with a hole in the center and used a plunger. As we worked the plunger up and down, the cream would turn to butter. The butter was washed with cold water and then salted.

We had a wooden butter press. It also had a plunger, a round bottom cup and a cover that had a leaf design with a hole in it. We would fill the cup up with butter, press it in solid, and push a plunger. Out would come a perfect pound of butter.

We had a one-room school house. The teacher taught all eight grades. In the winter, the school was heated with a large wood stove.

The school had a closet type room that was the library. There were not enough books for all students. So, to get a book, we would have to get to school early.

There were no buses. We would walk two miles to school. We carried our lunches in tin pails. Most of the time, we would have syrup or molasses sandwiches. In the winter, our lunch would often be frozen when we got to school. We were allowed to put our lunch by the stove. If we forgot and left it in the hall, we would eat it just the same.

In the summer we wore gingham dresses. The roads were so muddy that shoes did not wear well and we mostly went barefoot. Little streams ran across the roads. Mud was *sinky*. It was fun jumping up and down with our bare feet in the mud. It was as close as we came to a trampoline.

In the winter, we had dresses made from outing flannel. We also wore heavy underwear and capes or coats. Girls as well as boys wore lumberjack high top rubber boots with black stockings and wool socks. It was fun to wear them, but they were very hot in school.

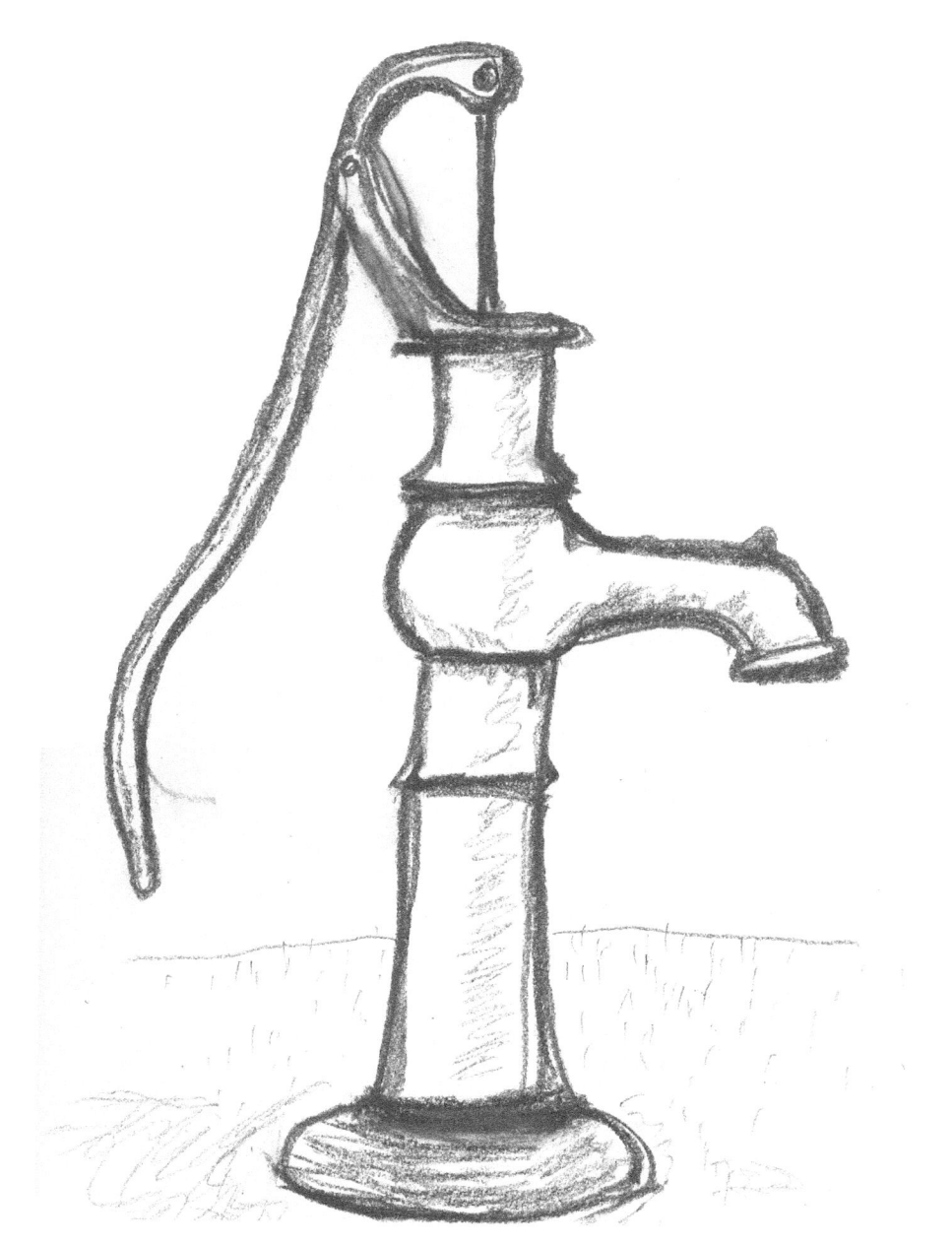

We had running water — we had to run for it. The boys had to help dad cut and chop logs. We girls had to carry in the firewood.

When we got old enough, there were chores in the barn: Milking, feeding and watering the cattle. We had to pump the water and many times it was too cold for the cows to drink.

We did not have many toys.

It was fun playing in the hay loft, sliding down on the stacks of hay.

Our school house was on a hill. With our home-made sleds we could coast a long way. It was an effort to get back up. But it was fun sliding down again.

Our brothers would make sleds and we would hook up three sleds and go! Our skis were made of curved barrel boards. We put a strap across the board over our lumberjack rubber boots and away we went.

Lumber men would haul logs with huge sleds, sometimes pulled by four horses. On Saturdays in the winter, after all our chores were done, we would catch a ride on top of the logs and ride until we met an empty sled coming back. We would keep this up for hours. Great grandpa would give a whistle on his fingers, and that was it. We headed home.

There was very little done on Sundays.

We finally got horses of our own including a small horse named Dora. We had a four-runner sleigh called a cutter. In it, we placed straw and blankets to keep us warm. We crawled onto the cutter and kept quiet. Great grandfather was very strict.

Great grandfather had a mustache. By the time we got to our friends he would have icicles on his mustache. We would fight over which of us would pull the icicles off of his moustache.

Great grandpa built the family a two-room log house. One room belonged to the cows. We can visit the cows without going out of doors. From the corner of one bed, we could peek around the door and see a cow having a baby calf. Mother chases us back. We are not to see this. After all, the stork brings the babies.

Besides the two sons, the stork brought mother three girls.

Dad and brother are in logging camp. Boys were taken out of school at thirteen and younger to go to work. Great grandma works very hard. My sisters and I now sew and chop our wood.

In the spring we are getting our field work ready. We stay home to help.

One thing we were blessed with is plenty of stones. When great grandfather plows, we follow the plow and pick up stones. We go barefoot because shoes will wear out too fast. Our feet can take it!

In the fall, we again stay out of school to pick and dig potatoes. It is fun getting the old root house ready to store away the vegetables. It is so dark inside. Sacks and sacks of potatoes are dumped in. My little kitten follows inside and a sack of spuds is dumped on it. No more kitten. I cried all day.

We have kerosene lamps. If we run out of kerosene, the old wood stove gives us light. We sing songs and play hide and seek. Great grandfather can play an accordion, clarinet and also a leaf and mouth organ. And he never had a music lesson.

We are tired and love to go to bed. Four of us would go in the same bed to keep warm. Our mattress is made of feed sacks and filled with straw. We can feel the cold from the bottom of the bed.

A few skunks make a home under our house. There are woodchucks and porcupines nearby. Rover had a fight with a porcupine and he is full of needles. It was like a game to pull out all the stickers.

We hear owls hooting and it feels scary.

It is spring and out comes the skunk with all the baby skunks. Rover chases her into the woods and he comes back — paid in full with a stinky scent.

Snow is melting and trees are starting to bud. Now is the time to find pussy willows.

It is fun to tap the maple trees. The juice runs out and tastes so sweet. We also look for gum on the tamarack trees. That keeps us quiet for a while. We chew the gum for a long time and spit a lot before it tastes good. Sometimes, we would find wintergreen leaves to add flavor.

We would find pine wood and make arrows. Pine wood was easy to cut. We had to find the right kind of branches to make the bows.

It is raining. We have no chores and we are going fishing. We walk past beautiful rivers and trees. The falling rain makes noises. We are still far off from the river with a long way to walk. There are three deer. They sail over a fence. How graceful and beautiful they are.

We have a swimming spot surrounded by a lot of trees. There is another place where the boys can swim. In a few minutes, our clothes are hanging on a limb and we are having fun.

Our black dog Topsy is acting peculiar. She gobbles her food and runs off. Let's watch to see what she is up to.

She runs through the high grass and disappears into the woods. After following her for several days, we found her in a pile of brush with three black babies and one puny brown baby with a short rabbit tail.

One little white chicken also gobbled her food and went away.

Great grandma said, "She must have a nest somewhere." Sure enough, here she comes clucking and leading home her little chicks.

Now the frogs start up. It is fun to catch them. The roads are wet and muddy. In the ditches are pollywogs. These are fun to handle, how they wiggle and slip through my hands.

We pick mayflowers and violets to bring them to great grandmother.

It is getting dark and we hike back home.

Appendix: Copy of letter from the 6th grade class at Moorhead State College Campus School, circa 1961:

Dear Parents and Grandparents:

We are interested, in our study about pioneers in Minnesota, in learning more about our first settlers here. Will you tell us about how life was when you were our age or stories your parents or grandparents told you?

1. Much of our time is spent in watching television or listening to the radio or going to school. How did you spend your time?

2. We wonder what you had to eat. Did you have fruit and vegetables? How did you keep your food from spoiling? Did you make your own butter?

3. Since there were not planes and no cars, how did you travel or go to visit friends?

4. Many of us have chores or duties at home. What did you have to do?

5. What were homes like? How were they heated and lighted?

6. We have so many library books, newspapers and magazines to read. What did you have?

7. In newspapers even a few years old, clothes look strange to us. How did you dress?

8. Can you tell us about any other pleasure or hardships of early days?

www.ingramcontent.com/pod-product-compliance
Lightning Source LLC
Chambersburg PA
CBHW041125120626
46547CB00019B/2860